INTER*CORPSE*

Necrophilia: sexual attraction towards corpses including sexual intercourse

By RJ Parker, PhD

Criminologist, Author and Publisher

I0115859

"This is a work of nonfiction. No names have been changed, no characters invented, no events fabricated."

RJ Parker

INTER*CORPSE*

Necrophilia: sexual attraction towards corpses including sexual intercourse

By RJ Parker, PhD
Criminologist, Author and Publisher

ISBN-13: 9781987902563

Copyright and Published

by *RJ Parker Publishing*

Published in United States of America

Copyrights

Table of Contents

Monthly KINDLE HD FIRE Giveaway

***

Drawing each month on the 30th...

***

Enter to WIN
(No Purchase Necessary)

Click HERE   *http://www.rjparkerpublish-*
ing.com/Win-a-Kindle.html

Introduction

What is Necrophilia?

The word necrophilia is made up of the prefix 'necro' (relating to corpse/death) and suffix 'philia' (which stands for abnormal love for a specified thing). Thus, the term necrophilia refers to having a sexual attraction towards corpses that may or may not include sexual intercourse.

It has been claimed that Belgian physician Joseph Guislain used this word while discussing a relatively modern-day necrophile François Bertrand in a lecture given around 1850. A decade later, necrophilia as a term was further made popular by a psychiatrist Bénédict Morel who mentioned the same François Bertrand in his work.

Incidents in Ancient History

There have been numerous cases of necrophilia in the past. In the book *Histories,* Greek author Herodotus (c.484–425 BCE) mentioned that in Ancient Egypt, bodies of extremely attractive women were embalmed three to four days after death – a preventative measure after the discovery of an incident in which an embalmer had sex with a female corpse.

Likewise, the book *'The Corpse: A History'* by Christine Quigley, noted that Gilles de Rais (a leader in the French army) was said to have sexually violated the dead bodies of his victims.

Categorization of Necrophiles

According to the 5th edition of Diagnostic and Statistical Manual of Mental Disorders, when a person experiences frequent misery or deficiency in areas of function due to regular and intense sexual interest in corpses, the behavior can be diagnosed under Other Specified Paraphilic Disorder (necrophilia). The classification of necrophilia can be shown in 10 tiers:

1. *Role players:* People who get stimulated from imagining that their live partner is deceased during sexual activity,

2. *Romantic necrophiliacs*: People that cannot separate themselves with their lover's body, even after death,

3. *Necrophiliac fantasizers*: People that never have sex with a corpse but rather fantasize about it,

4. *Tactile necrophiliacs*: People that become sexually aroused by simply

touching or caressing a corpse. No sexual intercourse is performed in this tier,

5. *Fetishistic necrophiliacs:* People who strip clothes or detach specific body parts (e.g., penis or fingers) from a corpse for sexual purposes. No sexual intercourse is performed in this tier,

6. *Necromutilomaniacs:* People who masturbate while mutilating a dead body. No sexual intercourse is performed,

7. *Opportunistic necrophiliacs*: People who usually have no interest in necrophilia, but when they see an opportunity to commit it, they do,

8. *Regular necrophiliacs*: People who regularly commit sexual intercourse with corpses,

9. *Homicidal necrophiliacs*: People who first murder a person, then have sex with the victim's corpse, and

10. *Exclusive necrophiliacs*: People that can only perform sex with corpses, not living partners.

Statistics and Research

Curiously enough, incidents of necrophilia can be found in both humans and animals. Concerning humans, *Rosman and Resnick* studied 122 cases of necrophilia in 1989. These cases were divided into necrophiles who had a continued attraction to corpses (genuine necrophiles) and those who committed the act when they saw the opportunity (pseudo necrophiles).

It was found that out of the 122 cases, 92 percent were male and 8 percent were female. Among the genuine necrophiles, around 57 percent had access to corpses due to their occupation such as being a morgue assistant or a cemetery worker. The researchers suggested that one of the following reasons might cause necrophiliac behavior:

1. Experiences of low self-esteem, mainly due to a loss in life. They might have one or both of the following fears:

    - fear of rejection by others which causes a desire to have a sexual partner who is unable to reject them;

    - fear of the dead which they counter by turning it into a desire.

2. A fantasy of having sex with a corpse grows inside them. This feeling often develops after a person sees/deals with a dead corpse.

In their sample of genuine necrophiles, the authors stated that

- 68 percent were inspired by having a partner that is submissive (unresisting) and unrejecting;

- 21 percent by a desire to reunite with a lover;

- 15 percent had strong sexual attraction to corpses;

- 15 percent were motivated by a chance to eliminate isolation; and

- 12 percent had the wish to exercise power over a dead body. This was found in necrophiles having low self-esteem.

Nearly 50 percent of the cases were found to have a personality disorder in which around 11 percent of genuine necrophiles were declared psychopathic.

The Hong Kong Butcher

This title was given to Lam Kor-wan (born June 22, 1955) who committed atrocious crimes in the city of Hong Kong. Other titles given to him include The Jars Murderer, The Rainy Night Killer, and The Rainy Night Butcher.

Lam was a taxi driver by profession who targeted lone female passengers. He would abduct, subdue, and strangle these women to death using an electric wire. Then take them to his house to mutilate the bodies. It was discovered by the police that Lam used to bottle the sexual organs of his victims in Tupperware containers. The police reported that sexual organs of three females were kept in formalin (preservative) and stored in his apartment. It was because of this discovery that Lam was coined the name 'The Jars Murderer'.

During the investigation, the police found thousands of photos of female organs taken by Lam. These photos were taken at various stages of dissection, and some also included close-ups of female genitalia. Lam also filmed himself while performing sex with his fourth victim.

Lam Kor-wan lived with his family, even shared a room with his unsuspecting brother. He worked at night in order to keep his 'grave' acts hidden from the rest of his family members.

The police initially considered Lam's brother a suspect but later found him not to be involved. The corpses that were dismembered were disposed of in isolated areas of New Territories and on Hong Kong Island. Lam used his taxi to transport them to these locations and tried to keep it hidden, but the bodies were ultimately located.

Arrest

Lam was arrested on August 17, 1982, while returning to a Kodak shop in Hong Kong where he left some photographs to be developed. Plainclothes officers, who were given information about the content of the photos by the shop manager in Mong Kok regarding, conducted the arrest. The officers waited for him to return to pick up his pictures, then confronted him.

Lam told the officers that the photographs did not belong to him, but rather to a friend. He also told them that his friend would be coming over to meet him. After no sign of Lam's friend, the police escorted him to his home on Kwei Chau Street and conducted a thorough search.

An ammunition box was found in his bedroom that contained pornographic images of victims, some videos and female sex organs stored in Tupperware containers.

The Four Female Victims

The four female victims of Lam Kor-wan include:

- Chan Fung-lan, age 21, whose corpse was dismembered in seven parts and was found in the Shing Mun River in New Territories,

- Chan Wan-kit, age 31, whose body was found in a rice bag near Tai Hang Road, Hong Kong Island,

- Leung Sau-wan, age 29, whose body was found in a rice bag near Tai Hang Road, Hong Kong Island, and

- Leung Wai-sum, age 17, whose body found in a rice bag near Tai Hang Road, Hong Kong Island.

Although there were four female victims that have been officially identified in this case, it is stated in an interview of a former journalist known only as "OCTB Sir Wong" that the police found fifteen bodies during the investigation (all female) that were a part of Lam's photo collection. Since they could only identify four, the case states only the above names could be used for prosecution. These victims were identified using the technique of photo-superimposition conducted by two expert lecturers from Prince Philip Dental Hospital.

Trial

After a trial lasting three weeks, Lam was found guilty of murder on four counts and was sentenced to death by hanging on April 8, 1983. However, Lam's sentence was converted to life imprisonment on August 29, 1984, as was the custom prior to the ending of the death penalty in Hong Kong in 1993.

Currently, Lam Kor-Wan is at the maximum-security prison facility at Shek Pik serving his sentence. During his discussions with psychiatrist Dr. William Green, Lam related that he "ate part of the intestine of one of the victims". Dr. Green said: "Lam was obsessed with female sex organs, but his curiosity, although having a sexual element, was not motivated by lust", while declaring "it was God who told him to kill the victims."

The Green River Killer

Gary Leon Ridgway (known as the Green River Killer) is a serial killer from the United States who has been found guilty of 49 murders, confessed to 71, but suspected to have killed more than 90 people. Ridgway was originally convicted of 48 killings, but the number rose to 49 following a plea bargain. This made him USA's serial killer with the highest verifiable murder count.

Gary Ridgway was born in Salt Lake City, Utah, on February 18, 1949, to Mary and Thomas Ridgway. His life at home was rather distressful, as stated by his relatives, with Gary's mother being described as bossy. His parents habitually argued in front of him in a violent manner, and this affected his behavior as well. Gary's dad frequently complained and was concerned about the number of sex workers in the city. During his teenage years (age 16), Gary led a six-year-old boy into the woodlands and stabbed him; luckily the boy was saved.

After graduating from Tyee High School in 1969, Ridgway joined the U.S. Navy and served on a supply ship. He experienced warfare after being sent to fight in the

Vietnam War. He married Claudia Kraig (aged 19) who was his girlfriend in high school. Despite his marriage, Gary had sexual intercourse with a lot of sex workers during his military career. He continued to have unprotected sex even after contracting gonorrhoea. Gary's marriage ended within a year after his extramarital affairs was discovered while he was away serving.

Ridgway was described by his friends and relatives as weird in behavior but also very friendly. His first two marriages ended after infidelity by both partners. Marcia Winslow (Gary's second wife) admitted to once being put in a chokehold by Gary. She also stated that he became very religious; reading the Bible, preaching to individuals, and convincing his wife to follow their pastor's teachings. He also cried while listening to sermons and reading the Bible. Despite his religious teachings, during his marriage, Ridgway did not keep himself away from obtaining the services of sex workers. He often urged his wife to have sex in the woods or at public places; in some places that he mentioned, bodies of victims were later found.

According to women throughout his life, Ridgway had a voracious sexual craving. His three ex-wives and a few ex-girlfriends revealed that Ridgway requested sex from them a few times each day. Frequently, he would need to engage in sexual relations in an open area or in the forested areas. Ridgway himself confessed to having an obsession with sex workers, with whom he had a love-hate relationship. As often as possible, he griped to others about their presence in his neighborhood; and yet, he availed of their services routinely. It has been hypothesized that Ridgway was torn between his wild desires and his staunch religious convictions.

Ridgway met Judith Mawson (his third wife) in 1985 at a function named 'Parents without Partners'. Judith was impressed of him being a gentle person and also admired him because of his 15-year job as a truck painter. Before moving her into his new house, Ridgway renovated the house and also changed the carpet. Judith was a bit different from Marcia; she admired her mother-in-law's habit of looking after any purchasing requirements and tasks like checking his account (these were seemingly difficult for Gary). Later on, these responsibilities were taken over by Judith.

When interviewed in prison by Pennie Morehead, Gary revealed that he truly loved Judith and, of his fondness towards her, he reduced his rate of murders. Statistics suggest that only 3 out of 49 victims were murdered after his marriage to Judith. During an interview, Judith told a local TV reporter, *"I feel I have saved lives...by being his wife and making him happy."*

During the 1980s and through to the 1990s, Ridgway is known to have killed no less than 71 females close to Seattle and Tacoma, Washington. In 2001, Ridgway himself admitted to this in a meeting with Sheriff Dave Reichert. His testimony in court later revealed that he had murdered such a large number of people even he forgot the exact number. The majority of the killings happened between the years 1982 and 1984. His victims were either sex workers that were pimped along Pacific Highway South (International Blvd. 99) or runaways.

A large number of his victims were dumped in lush regions around the Green River, with the exception of two affirmed and another two presumed casualties found in the Portland, Oregon region. The bodies were frequently left in groups at his dumping sites, some of the time postured, and generally naked.

Ridgway would occasionally come back to the dead bodies and have sex with them. Regardless of the stage of decomposition, he still engaged in necrophilia behavior. Some of the corpses were rolling in maggots while he had sex with them. Ridgway later explained that for him, he didn't discover necrophilia all the more sexually fulfilling, but engaging in sexual relations with the corpses diminished his need to get a live body. He rationalized that this restricted his chances of exposure and getting caught. Since the vast majority of the bodies were not found until only the skeletons remained, three victims are to this day unidentified.

In attempts to impede police investigations, Ridgway would pollute his dumping sites with gum, cigarettes, and composed materials owned by others. He even transported a couple of victims' remains across state lines into Oregon.

Ridgway started each murder by picking up a female hitchhiker, sharing or displaying a photo of his child to the female to deceive her into having confidence in him, and then overpowering her once her defences were down. After he raped his victim, he would choke her from behind. He learned his lesson about choking from the front after receiving wounds and injuries on his arms from his victims while they fought back. He was worried that people would ask where he got those wounds and injuries, so Ridgway started using ligatures. Ridgway's preferences of location for his murderous crimes were his own home, his truck, or an extremely secluded area where rarely one comes or goes.

To conduct research regarding the murders, the King County Sheriff's Office formed the Green River Task Force at the start of 1980s. Members of the elite team included Robert Keppel and Dave Reichert. They interviewed Ted Bundy about this UnSub and Bundy actually offered assistance and opinions as to what Ridgway must have been thinking, his behavior, and his possible next move.

Bundy advised the officers that whenever they found a grave of a freshly buried corpse, they should stake it out and sit tight, waiting for him to return. Bundy was of the opinion that Ridgway would return to have sex with the corpses that he murdered. Well-known FBI Special Agent John E. Douglas was also a major contributor to the Green River Killer investigation.

Ridgway was arrested and charged twice for engaging the services of sex workers - in 1982 and 2001. It was initially reported that he had passed a polygraph test about certain murders, but it was later discovered (after FBI review) that he had actually failed it. So in 1987, hair and saliva samples were collected by the police, which, after a DNA investigation, formed the basis for a bench warrant. Ridgway was arrested on November 30, 2001 at the Kenworth Truck Factory where he was working as a spray painter. He was held as a potential suspect and person of interest for the 20-year-old murders of four women, after matching the semen found in the corpses with the saliva sample taken by the officers. At that time, the four known victims were Marcia Chapman, Cynthia Hinds, Opal Mills, and Carol Ann Christensen; but the indictment increased by three more victims after microscopic spray paint spheres of a specific composition were found that were used at the Kenworth factory.

Confessions, plea bargain and sentencing

According to Seattle TV, in August 2003, Ridgway was moved to Airway Heights Minimum-Medium Security Level Tank from a maximum-security cell at King County Jail. Meanwhile, other news channels reported that the lawyers of Ridgway were closing in on a plea bargain that would allow Ridgway to escape the death penalty. This was subject to his confession of his full murder count.

Ridgway entered a plea bargain in November 2003 to 48 charges of first-degree murder. As a result of the plea, he was spared the death penalty, provided the details of his victims, and advised the investigation team the locations of his victims' remains. In the statement given by Ridgway, all the women were murdered within the limits of King County, Washington. He also disclosed that, to confuse the police, he dumped the remains of two women near the vicinity of Portland,

Oregon.

Deputy prosecutor Jeffrey Baird stated in court that the names of 41 other victims could not have been identified without the plea agreement. In his decision to make this deal, King County Prosecuting Attorney Norm Maleng explained:

"We could have gone forward with seven counts, but that is all we could have ever hoped to solve. At the end of that trial, whatever the outcome, there would have been lingering doubts about the rest of these crimes. This agreement was the avenue to the truth. And in the end, the search for the truth is still why we have a criminal justice system ... Gary Ridgway does not deserve our mercy. He does not deserve to live. The mercy provided by today's resolution is directed not at Ridgway, but toward the families who have suffered so much..."

Richard Jones, Superior Court Judge of King County, announced his decision to sentence Ridgway to 48 life sentences without parole; this decision was made on 18 December 2003. In addition to the 48 life sentences, one additional life sentence was to be served sequentially. Later, his sentence was increased to 10 additional years after he was found tampering with evidence relating to the victims.

In 2003, the locations of three bodies were disclosed by Ridgway; Pammy Annette Avent, a 16-year-old girl found close to State Route 410, Marie Malvar, and April Buttram.

In 2005, a weekend hiker was reported to have found the skull of one of the 48 victims. Another skull was found near Highway 18 southwest of Seattle by a hiker. This victim was believed to be Tracy Winston who was reported missing since 1983.

Ridgway confessed to 48 murders over a span of five months of investigation by the police and interviews by prosecutors. Out of these, 42 were already probable victims of Ridgway. In 2004, the videotape records of Ridgway's confessions began to be made public by the county prosecutors. Ridgway's confession of murdering 65 women was found in one of the videotapes. In another taped interview, he told the investigators that he was responsible for the murder of 71 women. He further disclosed that he had sexual intercourse prior to murdering them. Ridgway stated that his victims were mainly sex workers because of his hatred towards them, and it was also much easier for him to pick them up. After some time had passed, he admitted to wanting to end his thirst of necrophilia; therefore, he buried the next victims.

Before murdering the victims, he wanted to calm them down; *"I would talk to her... and get her mind off of the, sex, anything she was nervous about. And think, you know, she thinks, 'Oh, this guy cares'... which I didn't. I just want to, uh, get her in the vehicle and eventually kill her."* He then later stated that killing young females became his 'career'.

At the start of 2004, Gary Ridgway was placed in solitary confinement at Washington State Penitentiary but was later transferred to USP Florence, a federal prison close to Cañon City, Colorado. In order for Ridgway to be "easily accessible" by investigating officers, it was announced by Corrections Secretary Bernie Warner that he would be moved back to Washington. On October 24, 2015, Ridgway was transferred by plane to Washington and there he remains.

Edmund Kemper

Edmund Kemper, born in California, United States, on December 18, 1948, is an American serial killer. Kemper committed his first murders at the age of 15, and during 1964-1973, the murder count went up to ten. He also frequently participated in necrophilia and once stated that he ate the flesh of one of his victims. However, the admission of cannibalism was later withdrawn.

Kemper's grandmother, Maude Matilda Hughey Kemper (1897–1964), became his first victim because of an argument that they had while sitting at the kitchen table. Kemper became furious; he picked up his .22 caliber rifle and shot her in the head. Two more shots were fired on her back and multiple stab wounds were also discovered in the post-mortem report. Kemper later shot his grandfather, Edmund Emil Kemper, in the driveway when he arrived home from purchasing groceries. He called his mother, told her about the incident, and then asked her what to do. She instructed him to call the police.

When the police arrived, Kemper was questioned regarding the murders. He told the authorities that he wanted to see what it felt like to kill his Grandma and that he had to murder his grandfather so he would not know that his wife was dead. According to court psychiatrists, Kemper was suffering with paranoid schizophrenia. Kemper was sent to Atascadero State Hospital and admitted to its unit for the criminally insane.

At Atascadero State Hospital, psychiatrists of California Youth Authority completely disagreed with the diagnosis made by court psychiatrists. They insisted that Kemper displayed "no flight of ideas, no interference with thought, no expression of delusions or hallucinations, and no evidence of bizarre thinking". His IQ was initially recorded at 136, but later, while he was at Atascadero, he was reported to have an IQ of 145.

During his time in prison, Kemper portrayed himself as a good prisoner and administered psychiatric tests to other inmates. Kemper later revealed that he was able to manipulate his psychiatrists, as he understood the way the tests worked. He also stated that the sex offenders to whom he administered tests gave him tips. For example, ensuring he murdered the woman after committing rape to avoid leaving proof or evidence behind.

Kemper was released from the hospital, supposedly cured, and later went on a murder spree. Between May 1972 and April 1973, Kemper killed five female college students, one high school girl, his own mother and her best friend. During these 11 months, he committed degrading acts with all his victims such as sex, stabbing, mutilation, and strangulation.

In his interviews, Edmund Kemper has stated that he was compelled to commit murders after he had arguments with his mother. Kemper admitted that he and his mother, Clarnell Elizabeth Strandberg, had an extremely volatile relationship. During one of their arguments, she told him that she avoided introducing him to females at the university where she worked by saying, 'you're just like your father. You don't deserve to get to know them'. Hearing this contributed to his frustration and hate towards his mother. It is believed by psychiatrists that the young females he murdered were surrogates for his mother, the ultimate target.

Mary Ann Pesce and

Anita Luchessa

On 7 May 1972, Edmund picked up two 18-year-old hitchhiking students, Mary Ann Pesce and Anita Mary Luchessa while he was driving in Berkeley. The girls wanted a ride to Stanford University, to which Kemper agreed, but after driving for about an hour, he somehow managed to change his route towards an isolated area near Alameda without alerting the two girls. This place was well known by Kemper through his work at the Highway Department. After reaching his destination, he handcuffed Pesce and locked Luchessa in the trunk. He then later strangled Pesce to death and murdered Luchessa in a similar way.

Kemper initially had the idea of only raping them, but he remembered the advice of serial rapists at Atascadero who advised him to avoid leaving any proof or witnesses behind. In his confession, Edmund Kemper admitted that he "brushed the back of [his] hand against one of her breasts and it embarrassed [him]" while handcuffing Pesce, and also added "[he] even said 'whoops, I'm sorry' or something like that" after grazing her breast, even though he then murdered her moments later.

Kemper placed the bodies in the trunk and headed back to his apartment. On the way, he was stopped by a police officer but managed to avoid a search and got away with only an offence involving a broken taillight. Since his roommate was not home, he took the bodies to his room, posed them in order to take pornographic photos, and had sex with their corpses. He then dismembered their bodies and placed them in plastic bags to drop them off near Loma Prieta Mountain. Before dumping their remains off a ravine, Kemper committed one final act of necrophilia when he had irrumatio with the severed heads of both females. Pesce's skull was found three months later in August on Loma Prieta Mountain. The rest of her remains and that of her hitchhiking partner were not found even after an extensive search.

Aiko Koo

Aiko Koo was a 15-yearoold Korean dance student who missed her bus and decided to hitchhike to her dance class. It was the evening of 14 September 1972 when Kemper, merely by chance, was going her way, spotted her hitchhiking, and picked her up. Like before, he headed away towards a secluded area. Once parked and outside, he waved his gun at Aiko, but in the process, he found himself locked out of his own car. Aiko later allowed Kemper back in after gaining her trust. Back in the car, he choked her unconscious, raped and killed her. Kemper then put her body in the trunk of his car. On the way home, Kemper stopped and had a few drinks in a bar, not too far away from the crime scene. Brazenly, outside the bar, he opened his car's trunk, "admiring [his] catch like a fisherman," and returned home. After reaching his apartment, he committed sex acts and dismembered her body in the same way as he did with Pesce and Luchessa. Aiko Koo's mother placed hundreds of flyers around the town and reported to the police of her daughter's disappearance, but she received no response regarding her daughter's whereabouts or case status.

Cindy Schall

On 7 January 1973, Kemper picked up Cynthia Ann 'Cindy' Schall, a college student of age 18, while he was cruising around Cabrillo College. He ended up shooting her in the head with his .22 caliber pistol after reaching a remote region. He took her body to his mother's home (by now, Kemper was living again with his mother) and hid her body in his closet for the night.

The next morning, after his mother left, he took out the corpse and had sex with it. Kemper also removed the bullet from Cindy's body, dismembered it in his mother's bathtub, and kept her head for having irrumatio. He then later buried Cindy's head in the garden tilting her face front up towards his mother's bedroom. In the investigation held subsequently, Kemper remarked that his mother "always wanted people to look up to her." He managed to dispose of the rest of the remains by tossing them off a cliff. The search team found only her head and right hand a few weeks after the crime was committed. The police stated that Cindy's body had been sliced up into pieces with a power saw.

Rosalind Thorpe and Alice Helen "Allison" Liu

On 5 February 1973, Kemper, who was especially riled after an argument with his mother, left the house to continue his killing spree. By now the news of missing students was widespread, all the students who hitchhiked their way to the University were advised to accept a ride with only those cars that had a University sticker on them. Kemper had such a sticker as his mom worked there. While driving, he came across 23-year-old Rosalind Heather Thorpe and

20-year-old Allison Liu who accepted a lift in his car. He used his .22 caliber pistol again to shoot both girls and then wrapped the corpses in blankets.

This time Kemper brought back headless bodies to his mother's house to have sexual intercourse. He further mutilated their bodies, removed the bullets, and as soon as the sun rose the next morning, he prepared to dispose of the remains at Eden Canyon. A week later, the remains of the two girls were found.

In an interview, Kemper explained why he decapitated the heads before having sex: "The head trip fantasies were a bit like a trophy. You know, the head is where everything is at, the brain, eyes, mouth. That's the person. I remember being told as a kid, you cut off the head and the body dies. The body is nothing after the head is cut off ... well, that's not quite true, there's a lot left in the girl's body without the head."

Clarnell Strandberg and Sally Hallett

On the night of 20 April 1973, Kemper was falling asleep waiting for his then 52 year-old mother who was on her way home from a party. When she arrived, Kemper was awakened by the noise. She was reading a book in her bed when she saw Kemper approaching her and said, "I suppose you're going to want to sit up all night and talk now," to which Kemper replied "No, good night!"

Kemper waited for her to fall asleep, then returned with a claw hammer to slam into her face and a knife to cut her throat. After she was dead, he chopped her head off, performed irrumatio with it, and used it as a dartboard. Kemper stated that he "put [her head] on a shelf and screamed at it for an hour...threw darts at it," and finally, "smashed her face in." He went even further this time and cut her tongue out, as well as her larynx, and placed it in the garbage disposal. The disposal system was unable to break down the tough vocal cords to which Kemper remarked: "That seemed appropriate, as much as she'd bitched and screamed and yelled at me over so many years." He then had sex with her corpse and after hiding her in a closet went off to have a drink at a bar.

Meanwhile, Kemper invited his mother's best friend, Sara Taylor "Sally" Hallett, age 59, for dinner and to watch a film. When she arrived, he strangled her to death, chopped her head off and spent the rest of the night with her corpse. Kemper then hid her in a closet and wrote a note to the police reading:

Appx. 5:15 A.M. Saturday. No need

for her to suffer any more at the hands of this horrible "murderous Butcher". It was quick—asleep—the way I wanted it. Not sloppy and incomplete, gents. Just a "lack of time". I got things to do!!!

Edmund Kemper drove off in Hallett's car, exiting California to arrive in Pueblo, Colorado. When he did not hear any news regarding the crime scene and his note, he made a call to the police from a phone booth. The police took his call as a prank when he confessed to the murders of his mother and Sally Hallett. A few hours later, Kemper decided to call a police officer he personally knew. He told him that he killed his own mother and her friend and related his acts committed back at his mother's house. Kemper then waited for the police to come and arrest him. When they arrived, he also confessed that he murdered six female students.

When Kemper was asked to tell why he turned himself in to the police, he said: "The original purpose was gone ... It wasn't serving any physical or real or emotional purpose. It was just a pure waste of time ... Emotionally, I couldn't handle it much longer. Toward the end there, I started feeling the folly of the whole damn thing, and at the point of near exhaustion, near collapse, I just said to hell with it and called it all off."

On 7 May 1973, Edmund Kemper was

charged for the murder of eight persons of which all were females. Attorney Jim Jackson, Chief Public Defender of Santa Cruz County, was assigned to him; Jackson was previously assigned to the Herbert Mullin case involving John Linley. The only option left for the counsel was to plead not guilty by reason of insanity to the charges due to the fact of Kemper's open confession to the police. During his time in custody, Kemper twice tried to kill himself but failed both of the times. His trial was postponed to 23rd October 1973.

Kemper was declared sane by three psychiatrists appointed by the court. Dr. Joel Fort, one of the psychiatrists, found Kemper to be psychotic in his childhood by investigating his juvenile records. Fort kept Kemper under truth serum, interviewed him and reported to the court of Kemper's cannibalism, stating that he consumed the flesh of his victims. Kemper was found mindful during these interview sessions and liked being called a murderer. Kemper's confession of cannibalism was later rejected by him.

The M'Naghten standard was used by California which stated clearly that in order for a defendant to "establish a defense on the ground of insanity, it must be clearly proved that, at the time of the committing of the act, the party accused was laboring under such a defect of reason, from disease of the mind, as not to know the nature and quality of the act he was doing; or if he did know it, that he did not know what he was doing was wrong." In Kemper's case, he had already shown signs of malice aforethought, and it was believed that he knew that his acts were immoral.

On the 1st of November, Kemper told the jury that he was well aware of his unstable state of mind by describing how he felt sexually thrilled in beheading someone. He testified that the reason for murdering the victims was that he wanted them "for myself, like possessions." He also told the jury that he felt two beings inhabited his body; when the killer personality took over him, it was "kind of like blacking out".

The jury, comprised of six men and six women, declared Edmund Kemper guilty on November 8, 1973 after five hours of deliberation. Kemper requested the jury to give him the death penalty, "death by torture." At that time the Supreme Court placed a moratorium on capital punishment, so instead Kemper was given a life sentence for each murder count to be served at the same time (concurrently). He was then sentenced to the California Medical Facility for medical treatment and imprisonment.

Kemper's prison block was the same as that of other well-known serial killers and murderers such as Charles Manson and

Herbert Mullin. He looked down upon Mullin, who was also committing murders in Santa Cruz during Kemper's killing spree, and said: "He's just a cold-blooded killer ... killing everybody he saw for no good reason." In spite of this, Kemper remarked on his "self-righteous talking like that [about Mullin], considering what [he had] done." Mullin, at 5 feet 7 inches tall, was still intimidated by Kemper who was well over a foot taller than him. He also stated that "[Mullin] had a habit of singing and bothering people when somebody tried to watch TV, so I threw water on him to shut him up. Then, when he was a good boy, I'd give him peanuts. Herbie liked peanuts. That was effective, because pretty soon he asked permission to sing. That's called behavior modification treatment."

Kemper was regarded as a model prisoner among the overall prison inmates in 2015. He also became an excellent craftsman of ceramic cups and was given the duty of arranging appointments with psychiatrists for other prison inmates. Kemper's voice was recorded while he narrated books for the blind due to his exceptional reading skills. According to a Los Angeles Times article written back in 1987, Kemper was made the coordinator of the reading program and devoted more than 5,000 hours in narrating books.

Kemper appeared in a number of documentary interviews during his imprisonment, like The Killing of America, 1982, and in Murder: No Apparent Motive, 1984. These documentaries were famous for having an insight in the mind of serial killers and the way they operate. John E. Douglas, a special agent and unit chief in the FBI, described Kemper as having "rare insight for a violent criminal" and regarded him "among the brightest prison inmates" he ever interviewed during a criminal investigation.

Kemper himself stated that the reason for participating in the documentaries was to save others from murders. The last line of the documentary Murder: No Apparent Motive, Kemper said: *"There's somebody out there that is watching this and hasn't done that – hasn't killed people, and wants to, and rages inside and struggles with that feeling, or is so sure they have it under control. They need to talk to somebody about it. Trust somebody enough to sit down and talk about something that isn't a crime; thinking that way isn't a crime. Doing it isn't just a crime, it's a horrible thing, it doesn't know when to quit and it can't be stopped easily once it starts."*

Still, Kemper was reported to have displayed hostile behavior. One such incident happened with Robert Ressler, a colleague of John E. Douglas, during investigation in

Kemper's cell all alone. Robert was feeling nervous and uneasy and was repetitively hitting a button to call a guard. Kemper noticed the anxiety and said to him: "Relax. They're changing the shift," followed by, "If I went apeshit in here, you'd be in a lot of trouble, wouldn't you? I could screw your head off and place it on the table to greet the guard." Robert exchanged verbal blows with Kemper, who at that time weighed around 300 pounds and looked intimidating. Ressler responded, "Wouldn't you get in trouble for that?" Kemper replied, "What would they do, cut off my TV privileges?" Luckily, Robert exited the cell with no damage. Kemper later told him that he was just kidding. However, it then became a policy for FBI to enter Kemper's cell, and all other serial killers' prison cells, in pairs.

In 1979, Kemper first became eligible for parole, but it was not given to him that year. He was also denied parole in the years 1980, 1981 and 1982 at his parole hearings. Kemper then gave up his right to parole hearings of 1985, 1988, 1991, 1994, 1997, 2002 and 2007 on the belief that he was not suitable to come back and live in society. In the parole hearing of 2007, attorney Scott Currey said that Kemper is "happy going about his life in prison" and that Kemper is certain that nobody is going to award him parole. In 2012, he said that he was least concerned regarding his attendance in the hearing to be held in 2017, in which Kemper was again denied parole. He will be eligible again in 2024.

Female Cases of Necrophilia

Karen Greenlee

Karen Greenlee was born in 1956. She worked at the Memorial Lawn Mortuary in Sacramento, California, as an apprentice embalmer. On December 17, 1979, she was driving a 1975 Cadillac hearse to a funeral that she later stole along with the corpse of a 33 year-old man. As detailed in a movie based on the story of Greenlee, she reached the place of the funeral, and as she saw the family of the deceased, she "did a big donut and took off". Some days later, she was found near Alleghany in Sierra County. After examining and pumping Karen Greenlee's stomach, Dr. Robert Rocheleau said that she overdosed on 20 pills of Tylenol and codeine intending to commit suicide but survived. A four-page written confession was later found with her possessions. She confessed that she had had sex with 20 to 40 other corpses of young males and called it her "addiction".

In this event, Greenlee was only indicted and found guilty of stealing the hearse. Since necrophilia was not illegal in California at that time, she could not be charged. She was sentenced to jail for seven days and had to pay a fine of $255. When she was released, she received therapy that proved effective in bringing her peace.

Marian Gonzales, the mother of John L. Mercure, the victim, sued Karen Greenlee and Memorial Lawn Mortuary for $1 million for "severe emotional distress". The defense psychiatrist, Dr. Captane Thomson, stated at the Superior Court hearing that the event did not have "much of a lasting impact" on Marian. He believed this due to Marian's past records of depression and alcoholism. Richard A. Kapuschinsky, who was a fellow embalmer and coworker of Greenlee, defended her by describing her as skilled and easygoing and said "there was no reason to suspect" her. In the end, the lawsuit was settled for $117,000.

In 1987, a few years after the incident, Greenlee shared her story in a very detailed and open way to Jim Morton regarding her necrophiliac behavior. Her interviews, under the title 'The Unrepentant Necrophile', were made a part of Morton's book, Apocalypse Culture. Greenlee disclosed her attraction towards young males, the things she used to do with their corpses, along with her desire for the smells of death and human blood. Later on, she was unhappy that she gave the interview and moved to another city.

When Greenlee was asked about changing attitudes of people towards necrophilia, she replied: "Yeah, when I came out here, I noticed it. It's almost a fad! They're not really necrophiles, but pseudo-necrophiles. Like a death cult! But there are probably a lot of people who would do it if they had the opportunity."

The story of Greenlee was included in Barbara Gowdy's "We So Seldom Look On Love" in 1992 which further gave ideas to Lynne Stopkewich's Canadian film Kissed (1996). The main character in the movie was a young female embalmer who engaged in the practice of necrophilia. Molly Parker, the actress who portrayed the role of Karen Greenlee, earned the "Performance by an Actress in a Leading Role" award at the Genie Awards. In 1996, Greenlee was reported to have been travelling to America and sharing her story of necrophilia.

As per Esoterra, a culture and horror magazine, Sally Jessy Raphael conducted an interview of Greenlee but then later declined airing it as Greenlee showed no regret for her actions.

Louise Vermilya

L ouise Vermilya was a "black widow" who committed murders between late 19th century and the start of 20th century. Her murders were discovered after she began killing outside of her family. She always had an addiction towards corpses.

Louise Vermilya was born in 1868 to Prussian immigrants Wilhemina and John Woolf in Cook County, Illinois. Her name was Louesa Woolf at the time of her birth. The couple had 11 children of whom Louise was the third eldest and the eldest daughter out of five. When she reached the age of 16, Louise married 24-year-old Fred Brinkamp on the 2nd of April 1885. She then later moved to the village of Barrington in Lake County, Illinois.

Louise's homicidal killing started with the murder of her first husband, Fred Brinkamp, in 1893. The couple were residing on their farm close to Barrington, Illinois, when this incident took place. The reason for Brinkamp's death was declared by the coroner to be a heart attack. As the beneficiary, Louise inherited the proceeds from a life insurance policy amounting to $5,000. Since Brinkamp's age at the time of death suggested natural causes of death, no suspicions arose. There were six children of Fred Brinkamp that he left behind, two of whom faced similar experiences as their father later on.

According to Undertaker E.N. Blocks, owner of a mortuary in Barrington, Louise liked working around corpses and that she appeared too keen and excited to work with him in the mortuary. He said that she was not even a salaried employee but still came to work: "While I never employed her, for a couple of years I couldn't keep her out of the office," and that "at every death she would seem to hear of it just as soon as I, and she would reach the house only a little behind me."

In 1906, Louise moved to Chicago, and during her stay there, she took the life of Lilian Brinkamp, her 26-year-old stepdaughter. She got away with this murder as well as the coroner declared "acute nephritis" as the cause of her death. As the number of deaths increased, the Brinkamp family was thought of as being cursed.

Louise then later married 59-year-old Charles Vermilya. Seemingly ill, Charles died three years later. As his beneficiary, Louise inherited a home in Crystal Lake, Illinois, and cash amounting to $1,000. Shortly after Charles died, his son Harry Vermilya was murdered after having a fiery argument with

Louise over the sale of Crystal Lake estate. No one was suspected for any of these deaths, and the blame was put down to mere "coincidence".

Many others died at Louise's hand, but she got away every single time. Until the day everyone discovered Louise's gruesome act of poisoning people to get her hands on the life insurance proceeds. On 31st October 1991, Louise was busted at last during her failed attempt to commit suicide with an overdose of stolen arsenic. The overdose did not take her life but instead paralyzed her. Although Louise showed no regret for her actions, and in fact straight-out denied of all charges against her, the jury pitied Louise's physical and mental state and set her free.

Shockingly, later rumor had it that Louise, after poisoning her victims, would then sexually please herself with their corpses. Although it was not conclusively proven that Louise indulged in necrophilic activities, the testimony of the undertaker Blocks concerning her obsession with corpses and morgues indicates otherwise.

Juana "La Peque Sicaria"

Juana 'La Peque Sicaria' (the little killer) was a 28-year-old hitwoman for one of the most dangerous cartels in Mexico that went by the name of "Zetas". According to Mexican media, her association with the cartel came after some thugs murdered her brother. Juana was born in Hidalgo, Mexico, and became pregnant at the age of 15 by a man that was twenty years older than her. In order to provide support and financial assistance to her child and family, Juana headed towards prostitution.

In an interview from a prison in Baja, California, Juana said: 'Ever since I was a little girl I was a rebel, and then became a drug addict and an alcoholic.' According to Central European news, she told her story of starting her life of crime with the cartel as a lookout for patrols of police and army under the position of 'halconeo'. For eight hours a day, she would simply stand at a specific lookout point, and if she proved unsuccessful, she was given one taco per day and was tied up in a chair.

During her work for the Zeta Cartel, Juana witnessed and participated in horrific crimes. One of them was using a mace to smash open a man's head. 'I remember feeling sad and thinking I did not want to end up like that,' said Juana. But her dislike towards murder and blood was not long-term.

Denuncias, a local news site, stated that Juana engaged in necrophiliac and cannibalistic behaviors. Juana herself admitted to feeling "excited by it [blood], rubbing myself in it and bathing in it after killing a victim,' further stating, 'I even drank it when it was still warm.' Juana also 'insinuated' at having 'had sex with the corpses of those decapitated, using the severed heads as well as the rest of their bodies to pleasure herself.'

Other members of the Zeta Cartel were indicted for having used diesel fuel to cook their victim's flesh after chopping them up into pieces. Currently, she is imprisoned in a Mexican rehabilitation institution called Centros de Reinserción Social de Baja California. Juana is awaiting her sentencing, but confessions like these would not assist her case.

Victor Ardisson

For the quaint little-known French town called Le Muy, the 20th century started off on a disturbing note. Even for the rest of France and, later, the world, the news coming out of this town would be most shocking and disturbing. At the heart of the bizarre news was a man by the name of Victor Ardisson. Soon enough, he would become the embodiment of necrophilia.

It was 1901 when Honore Ardisson's (Victor's stepfather) neighbors started complaining about a foul smell coming from his house. At the time, only Honore was at home Honore was quick to dismiss the neighbors, saying that the smell must have been from the garbage disposal area. Curious though, Honore followed a peculiar odor to the attic of the house. In the dimly lit room, he stumbled upon something he thought was a dead animal. Upon closer inspection, the object was the body of a three-year-old girl.

Honore called the police immediately, who, upon quick investigation of the rest of the house, discovered more body parts and items. All indications were that the body and items therein had been stolen from a local cemetery. Without question, this bizarre discovery at his house saw Honore detained at the police station until further investigation. But after a shocking confession by Victor, Honore was released. It is this confession that would go viral. And even in 1901, the international media picked it up and shocked the world.

After being dispelled from the military, Victor Ardisson struggled to find work back in his hometown of Le Muy. When an opening for a gravedigger at the local cemetery came up, Victor and his stepfather were hired. However, his stepfather suffered an accident after he fell inside a grave he had dug. Victor took over the grave digging work on his own.

In addition to digging graves, Victor was also the town's undertaker, closely handling many bodies. Having ready access to corpses made it very easy for him to fulfill his darkest desires. And Victor's desire was to have sex corpses.

Victor admitted to always having an attraction to corpses, and then later, this attraction led him to want to have actual sex with the bodies. At the end of the interview, Victor confessed to having sex with over 100 bodies in the town of Le Muy.

Victor also admitted to mutilating the bodies after having sex with them in some cases. He abused the bodies he was in care of as an undertaker, and he also exhumed already buried bodies for abuse. Mainly females, but his attraction was not restricted by age.

As if this was not shocking enough, Victor also admitted to talking to the dead bodies in hopes that they would reply. The body of the three-year-old girl that was found at his stepfather's house was particularly special to Victor. He used her body for oral sex. He believed that through his acts, he would bring her back to life. Victor confessed that he thought that through his actions, the bodies would revive.

Victor would refer to the victim's bodies as 'brides' when he abused them. In some cases, he would refer to them as 'my fiancee' and kiss them passionately as if they were alive.

This horrendous confession sent chills through the spines of many. Victor was charged with innumerable counts of grave robbing, abuse of corpse and necrophilia.

As a result of this strange confession, some experts like Dr. Alexis Epaulard compared and likened necrophilia to vampirism. His behavior earned Victor the nickname 'Vampire of Muy'. While investigating the case, Victor underwent many mental evaluations, and many specialists were called in.

Victor was arrested and confined to

the Draguignan jail where the authorities debated whether he was sane enough to stand trial.

This ghastly story out of Le Muy, however, brought more questions than answers. Specifically, many were curious about Ardisson's upbringing and childhood and whether something happened that manifested into this disturbing behavior.

Victor was born in 1872 to a single mother. His real father remained a mystery only his mother knew. Soon after, Victor's mother married Honore Ardisson. During the investigation, Honore revealed the rocky childhood that Victor went through. According to the stepfather, Victor's mother was very abusive, striking him across the head with great brutality at times. In fact, there is speculation that some of his mother's blows may have affected his mental abilities.

One day Victor's mother decided to leave and Honore was left to care for Victor. Of course this abandonment would have played a key role in Victor's development. Victor was a loner in school. Other children constantly teased him, and when he reached his teens, things only got worse. In the village of Le Muy, he and his stepfather had a reputation for petty crime. For this reason, many people snubbed them in general.

Victor's social interactions were anything but normal. In his village, he would oddly follow females to public restrooms. It is said that he spied on girls while they urinated. In some cases, he would try to gather the urine and drink it. This disturbing tendency did not seem to bother him at all. In fact, it was noted that he was never depressed or down. Always cheerful and upbeat, Victor was ignorant of the jeers and pranks directed his way by others. In a way, he lived in his own cocoon and could have been numb to a lot of backlash.

Victor's interactions with girls were limited. Besides oddly following them around, whenever he tried to talk to them, he was laughed at. It was said that his only sexual encounters were with prostitutes and beggars who were brought home by his stepfather. Suspicions, and sometimes evidence, that he was a deeply perverted individual didn't help. It was said that he had a tendency to masturbate publicly. Victor also had other disturbing practices like drinking his own semen. In his own words, "it was a pity to let it go to waste." Obviously, Victor had a real hard time understanding social norms and interacting with live people.

When it came to looking for jobs, options were limited in Le Muy. He considered enlisting in the army, which he did, but other soldiers would often abuse him. This resulted in him deserting his duties a couple of times. Finally, he was discharged from the military owing to his inconsistency. At this point, he went back to his village and got the grave-digging job.

After the news broke out in the village and in the country, devastated family members of people who had been buried in the graveyard were in shock. There was a need to find out whether their beloved departed had been defiled posthumously. The town was in an uproar.

The report on Victor's psychiatric analysis remains a classic. Dr. Epaulard described Victor as a 'degenerate impulsive sadist necrophile'. The specialist was also keen to notice some facial features regarding Victor. He noted facial asymmetry as a big indicator of compromised intelligence. This went to reinforce this expert's conclusion that this necrophile might have been born this way.

However, in psychology circles, this is still one of the most prominent cases. William Stekel, a renowned psychoanalyst, was one of the last experts to talk to Victor. According to Stekel, Victor expressed his fondness for eating rats and cats. Stekel also noted that the only thing Victor feared was having his penis cut off. In the end, Stekel was able to conclude that Victor Arkisson was suffering from low intelligence with a form of sexual infantilism.

According to the investigations carried

out on his case, Victor was found to have very low upper body strength. It is this lack of strength that discouraged him from carrying larger bodies from the cemetery. It would also explain why he had a 3-year-old girl's body at his house and a teenager's skull in his custody. If he could not carry his entire corpse, he would carry a part of it.

After all the details and mental evaluations that had been done, it was clear that Victor seemed to have little comprehension of his crimes. During his trial, Victor would laugh or giggle at inappropriate moments. It was quite apparent to the prosecution that he was hopelessly insane. To this end, the court was reluctant to send him to the gallows. In an interview with a top psychiatrist, Victor revealed some inner fantasies that he had grappled with or entertained. In a way, it seemed like wishful thinking because, in some cases, Victor spoke as if he had actualized the fantasies. One of those disturbing fantasies was his desire to have sex with his mother's corpse. Victor also claimed to have earned money while selling his body to the men in his little village of Le Muy.

At the end of the trial, Victor was found not guilty by reason of insanity. The judge sentenced him to spend the rest of his life in a psychiatric hospital. After his sentencing, he did not have any sense of remorse for what he did. In fact, some experts who examined him concluded that he was happy to be getting free meals at the facility. Also, he was pleased by the fact that he could smoke freely. Victor was also impressed that he had achieved international notoriety. Indeed, he had put Le Muy on the map, albeit for the wrong reasons.

In March 1944, while in custody, Victor Ardisson died of natural causes at the psychiatric hospital where he had been incarcerated. He was given a proper burial at the same cemetery he had abused for such a long time.

The case of Victor Ardisson managed to horrify many, especially the people in his village. With a population of over 10,000 people today, Le Muy is known for its medieval architecture. It also has the Liberation Museum. After his death in 1944, people there preferred to forget all about Victor Ardisson.

Kaoru Kobayashi
Cold Blooded Pedophile

At around midnight, a motorist in Heguri in Nara Prefecture, Japan, noticed something in a roadside ditch. Upon closer inspection, the motorist discovered the barefoot body of a young girl. It was November 2004 when Kaede Ariyama was reported missing by her mother. As a student at a local elementary school, the 7-year-old girl was supposed to pick up her bike from home and head back to school. When hours passed without a word from the young girl, the parents notified the police who instituted a major search in the local area. The search encompassed more than 100 policemen, and this search ended when the motorist in Heguri found a body.

This dreaded news was delivered to Kaede's parents who broke down with sorrow. This was their first-born child. For months, the news dominated local headlines, but the real identity of the minor was kept hidden. However, the mourning family decided to reveal the identity of the girl in 2006 after the suspect's trial had began. The suspect had confessed to his crimes.

In December 2004, Kaoru Kobayashi was arrested as the main suspect for the sexual assault and murder of 7-year-old Kaede. Kobayashi had used the victim's mobile phone to send a photo of her dead body to his phone and an email to the victim's mother. This is how the police zeroed in on him as the main suspect. In addition, it was discovered that the suspect had also sent a threatening message to the girl's mother stating that he would come for her other daughter. Upon raiding his home, the police found crucial evidence against him including an assortment of child pornography, Kaede's cellular phone and other items. A stack of stolen girls underwear was also found at his house. According to an eyewitness report, the slain girl had been seen entering into the car of a strange man.

Upon arrest, it was discovered that Kobayashi was a multiple repeat offender. In fact, his criminal record was shocking. Born in 1968 to a poor family, he had to work as a paperboy to make ends meet. When he was 10 years old, he lost his mother. In 1989, he was arrested for sexually assaulting eight children. For these cases, he was sentenced for two years and a suspended sentence. Immediately after he got out of prison, in 1991, Kobayashi was arrested again and convicted for three years. His crime was an attempt to kill a 3-year-old girl. It was clear that this was a pedophile on the loose.

After being eligible for parole in 1995,

he was officially released from prison in 1996. After getting out of prison, he found a job in Ikoma-Tomio and worked as a newspaper deliveryman. It is at this period that the murder of the girl happened. On the 17th of November 2004, it is believed that Kobayashi took Kaeda hostage while on her way home to pick up her bike. The eyewitness at her school saw her enter his car. Investigators assume that she had been offered a ride. He then took her to his apartment where he sexually assaulted her. Then, the killer drowned her in a bathtub or sink. Investigators found that the water in the victim's lungs was clean water, pointing towards drowning in a tub.

Investigations revealed that after the ordeal, the killer dressed the girl's body before dumping it on a roadside ditch in Heguri. It was noted that some of her teeth were missing and that she had suffered some abrasions on the hands and feet. Her killer is believed to have mutilated and sexually molested the body after the drowning. According to some reports from the local bar, Kobayashi had shown off the pictures of Kaede claiming to have gotten them online. Some experts claimed that he killed her because she seemed intelligent enough to report him.

The trial officially began in April 2005. Kobayashi had confessed to his crimes. With little remorse on the case, he was quoted as saying that he wanted to be sentenced to death. His main drive for this was to leave a legacy just like fellow murderers Miyazaki and Takuma. These two were notorious pedophiles that had killed many children. Kobayashi went through psychiatric evaluation where the experts found that he was suffering from an antisocial disorder with pedophilia. However, he was found to be sane enough to face his actions. At some point, an expert stated that he had shown a little sense of guilt.

In September 2006, the Nara district court sentenced this killer to death by hanging. However, Kobayashi's defense was quick to appeal but then dropped the appeal. Kobayashi got a new lawyer who would continue with the appeal process in 2007. In 2008, the Osaka high court and the Supreme Court of Japan upheld the decision to execute Kobayashi through hanging. This pedophile breathed his last breath on February 21st, 2013, when he was executed by hanging at a detention center in Osaka.

Other crimes committed by Kobayashi

After the arrest had been made, a manager of a newspaper delivery agency the suspect had worked at came forth with some information. The manager had noted a stolen newspaper subscription fee that totalled 230,000 yen. The investigations at the time pointed to Kobayashi as the thief; he had, however, left the agency. On the same day he abducted the young girl, there was an arrest warrant issued by a judge for Kobayashi for the crime of embezzlement. The manager did not present the warrant to the police upon agreeing that Kobayashi would repay the money in monthly instalments. To this end, the suspect was not arrested that day and he went on to commit the murder.

The principal of the elementary school that the slain girl had attended expressed the hurt and trauma the school and parents had gone through. The news of the killer's hanging was welcomed, but it would not wipe away the sorrow. From that time, parents and guardians would accompany their children to and from the school. The local community was also shocked by the murder and, to many, this is a case that will linger in their memories.

The Otaku Connection

Before the arrest of Kobayashi, the local media had suspected an otaku connection with the murder case. Otaku refers to cultures and subcultures of people with obsessive interests, like manga fandom among a host of many others. A Japanese journalist made this connection after referring to the case of Tsutomu Miyazaki. Miyazaki was the notorious pedophile that was an otaku member. Kobayashi had idolized this murderer and wanted to follow in the same footsteps. In this respect, the journalist went further to suggest that the murderer could have been a member of the figurine collector's subculture.

However, after Kobayashi was arrested, it became clear that he was not a member of this subculture. In fact, his was a case of pedophilia that was not motivated by any ritualistic persuasions. All in all, the murder saw many otaku members targeted by authorities as the moral fiber of the country was tested. Otaku members were known for their erotic obsessions with materials such as erotic manga and video games. This case caused a political outcry where attention focused on making the streets and communities safer from pedophiles and other criminals.

The Kobayashi case inspired the passing of a law in Japan that is likened to Megan's Law in the United States. This is a law that requires the publication of all registered sex offenders and their locations. In other words, all sex offenders who have been in contact with the legal system must be known to the public for proper precaution and awareness by communities. Kobayashi was sent to the gallows alongside two other death row inmates. The Justice Minister at the time intimated that he had ordered the executions after considering the merits of the cases and orders given.

The execution of Kobayashi and two others led to a debate about capital punishment in Japan. Amnesty International Japan was quick to condemn the killings, referring to international human rights for all people. However, according to the opinion polls in Japan, as of 2013, around 80 percent of the population supported capital punishment. There was little information regarding the personal life of Kobayashi. It is not clear whether he had a girlfriend or he ever married. What became clear is that pedophilia defined most of his life, and it all ended with a gruesome murder of an innocent young girl. He was 44 years old when he was hanged and, by this action, one pedophile and murderer was cleared from the streets.

Anthony Merino

It remains well-known and understood that dignity is not lost when one dies. Your corpse may carry no life in it, but that is not to say that your body is free to be handled beyond the standard burial or cremation preparation. The only exception remains when you specify that you are donating your remains for scientific research or for organ transplants. Unfortunately, in 2007, a young Anthony Merino joined the growing list of individuals unfamiliar with this concept. On 28th of October, 24 year-old Anthony Merrino from New York City, was caught in the act of necrophilia – he was having sexual intercourse with a 92 year-old recently deceased woman in the morgue of a New Jersey hospital.

For a mere two weeks, Merino worked at the Holy Name Hospital in Teaneck, New Jersey as a Lab Technician. During this time he seemed like a regular employee. He also held a second part-time position at the Overlook Hospital in Summit, NJ as a Histology Technician. On the surface, he appeared to be a sound and hardworking young man. So when he told the guard at Holy Name Hospital that his key wasn't working and asked to be let into the morgue, the guard didn't hesitate.

Merrino lied to the guard, saying that he needed access to the morgue in order to inspect some sample tissue. The unsuspecting guard opened the morgue up for Merino before going about his work. But then reconsidering what he had done and sensing something was amiss, he returned to the morgue on his way back to check on things.

The guard walked in on Merrino sexually violating the body of a 92 year-old unnamed woman. Realizing he was caught, Merrino was desperately trying to get rid of the evidence by cleaning his genitals by the time the police showed up. Unfortunately for Merino, there was nothing he could do to evade arrest. Besides being caught with his "business" in his hands, there was an eyewitness to testify against him.

Merrino was charged with the desecration of the remains of a human being, which is considered a 2nd-degree offense in the state of New Jersey. He pleaded guilty and was sentenced to serve seven years in jail and received extensive psychiatric treatment while there. After a plea agreement, Merrino was released, however his whereabouts are not known. It remains unclear whether or not he was successfully treated for his condition.

There is not too much known about Merrino's childhood. Born in 1983 and living in New York City, Merrino was only 24 years old when we was arrested for necrophilia. Neither of his parents was in good health at that time. His father was suffering from colon cancer and his mother from Alzheimer's disease.

As information about his tenure at Holy Name Hospital emerged, it became obvious that Merino took the job to provide support for his parents, a humanly act from an otherwise twisted being. From all accounts, he seemed like a hard worker. He was only employed at the hospital for two weeks prior to the incident, but everyone said his work was fine and no one had any issues with him or his work. He also passed criminal background checks from both hospitals before being hired.

If you google Merino, you are likely to come across pictures of his blank stares and a face that showed almost no remorse for his actions. There has been no information uncovered as to whether the incident with the elderly woman was his first time or not.

There is no doubt that Merino was a necrophile, and while he is nowhere near as famous as criminals like Jeffrey Dahmer, he did send the state of New Jersey into a lengthy state of disgust and horror with his actions.

It seems like a common sense to lock people up for the crime of raping corpses, but unfortunately, not everyone agrees. In Merrino's case, for example, prosecutors argued that it was a medical condition that he could not control. In fact, other cases concerning necrophilia have some experts portraying perpetrators as victims of their own psychological urges, or even consider necrophilia as a sexual preference.

A few psychologists have argued in favor of treatment over punishment with some believing that extensive evaluation and therapy can lead to a change in behavior. This explains why Merino's sentence was not as severe as one would expect and why it was paired with mental health treatment. As bizarre as the idea of sleeping with a dead person may sound to the average human being, it's not unheard of and, in fact, many mental health experts have covered the condition in great detail.

Many people have argued that Merino's crime is not on the level of serial killers or murderers, and shouldn't be treated as such. Nor was he a previously convicted sex offender, but rather a man suffering from a condition he couldn't control.

On the far opposite side of the spectrum, some in Sweden support the notion of legalizing necrophilia, claiming people had the right to decide if their bodies could be used for sexual purposes after death or not. With such differing opinions, law enforcement has struggled to create solid laws to keep perpetrators in jail and, for now, many governments rely heavily on moral outrage and the degree of the crime to build strong cases against necrophiles. For Merino's case, the victim's body was defenseless, and he failed to present sufficient evidence to show that he acted out of temporary insanity. Other cases aren't so cut and dry.

Genzo Kurita: Japan's Game Changing Serial Killer

G ame changer is an accurate description of Genzo Kurita because he single-handedly managed to send the 1950s and, subsequently, 1960s Japanese society into complete shock and disarray. To be honest, even modern day global society is still both fascinated and disgusted by his cold, unforgiving and otherworldly sadistic feats.

But just who was Genzo Kurita? A remorseless serial killer, rapist, and necrophile who terrorized Japan's mothers and daughters until capture and subsequent hanging in 1959 would sum it up briefly.

However, psychologists have spent the better part of three to four decades trying to explain Kurita in more detail. Or how could he come to exist in the first place. And why so much hatred towards women and children? At this point, trying to figure out what went wrong during his individual development would be pure speculation, with suggestions ranging from childhood abuse, traumatic events in the World War II, to the plain and simple cruelty of a man who enjoyed preying on innocent mothers and their children. Either one could be true.

In his book, "Murder Under the Rising Sun: 15 Japanese Serial Killers That Terrified a Nation", author William Webb provided a probable theory that Genzo was drafted into the Imperial Japanese Army in 1944 when he was 18 years old. The Second World War was at its peak then and many men were left with no choice but to join the army. Soldiers of many wars have been tainted with the dark reputation of not only killing innocent civilians during combat, but also sexually abusing women and children in particular. In recent times, the UN troops in Africa and the Middle East have come under serious fire after investigations revealed countless cases of rape, sexual abuse and murder of civilians. Webb's theory is that it's possible that Kurita learned his vile ways when he was serving in during World War II. As probable as that is, it's still just a theory that has yet to be proven.

But if this theory is true, it would bring into question the level of efforts taken by all global governments to ensure that their soldiers and veterans are fully rehabilitated after combat and just how badly damaging war is exactly.

Reign of Terror

Throughout the course of his killing spree, one thing stood out about Kurita: he especially enjoyed hurting young mothers and their children. This could be linked to his own personal childhood, and there could be a deeper meaning behind his choice...a difficult relationship with his own mother perhaps? Again, it remains inconclusive, but it does not stop researchers from speculating and trying to make better sense of the murders.

During his first assault, he committed necrophilia with the corpse of a woman he just killed, while her baby was sleeping right next to her. During his second killing, a few months later, he threw a woman's three living children off the Osen Korogashi Cliff before raping and killing their mother. Miraculously, one child survived, but unfortunately, so did Kurita who continued his vicious attacks. It's not clear just how he performed the acts, but evidence showed signs of struggle on the victims' bodies in addition to bruises, cuts and other marks left behind by Genzo. His third murder in 1952 involved a woman and her niece. After the murders, he committed necrophilia with the niece's dead body.

Genzo finally broke his pattern in this final murder when his fingerprints were found all over the crime scene. As is the case with many serial killers, the challenge to remain anonymous and elusive becomes more difficult as their body count grows. It is almost inevitable that the killer will become more predictable as time goes by, and the authorities will be more familiar with their patterns. In other cases, once the killer feels like he has fulfilled his desires, he might purposely leave behind trails to help authorities catch him. Again, it depends on the state of mind of the killer and, again, there is no telling what was going on in their minds when they are committing their crimes.

One thing remains certain, Genzo's existence changed the perception of the death penalty in 1960s as well as modern day Japanese society. Prior to his arrest, many were against capital punishment, but as details emerged of his horrific assaults and his particular selection of victims, many people changed their beliefs in cases dealing with evil killers like Kurita.

It took two years for prosecutors to convince the courts that he deserved to be hanged for his crimes and that he met all necessary standards needed to qualify for the death penalty:

• First-degree murder, rape and necrophilia,

• Intent to cause grievous bodily harm and to kill,

• Committed the crimes in a cruel, calculated and obviously patterned manner,

• Possibility of there being more than

the recorded eight victims,

• Caused serious harm and trauma to surviving victims and family members,

• Had a grave and very negative impact on Japanese society, which spread terror amongst young mothers and children in particular,

• Was over the standard age of 18, which qualified him for the death penalty,

• Had a previous record of committing serious crimes which included the murder of two former girlfriends, and

• Showed no remorse and tried to plead insanity, which was immediately dismissed.

Kurita's killing sprees have sparked international interest by modern researchers and intellectuals who often compare his murders to that of another killer who took the USA by storm in the '70s, Ted Bundy. Much like Kurita, Bundy preyed on young women, although in his case, many of them resembled a former lover who had broken his heart. Bundy also targeted minors, but those incidents were isolated and in no way similar to Genzo's mother-and-child pattern.

One thing that stands out when comparing Kurita's killing spree to that of Ted Bundy is just how clear it is to see that Bundy was more elusive and, perhaps, even more disturbed than Kurita. Bundy's body count was believed to exceed 100 while Genzo's might have been somewhere between 8 and 20. This is not to undermine the gravity of Kurita's crimes but rather to acknowledge the evolution and sophistication of criminals after Genzo. In fact, many other killers emerged after him, and each seemed to double down on both the number of victims and the level of cruelty. There is no denying however, that Kurita brought to light a deeply disturbing fetish that was almost unheard of until then.

The mystery still remains as to just why Kurita began targeting innocent women and children, and the exact reason might never be known. He was, unfortunately, not a well-documented criminal, and if a movie was to be released or a book written about Genzo Kurita, it would be based purely off of speculation and theory about how he became to be such a twisted man. All that is known is that he will forever be a black stain in Japanese society that led to a dramatic shift in how people viewed capital punishment. He is one of the main reasons Japan still remains one of the few global nations to keep the death penalty in place. Even as global society evolves and human rights groups are actively campaigning against using the death penalty as punishment, cases such as Genzo Kurita's will always remind people that some criminals deserve no less than the harshest and most severe of all punishments. In some cases, it's the only way to achieve true justice. The only path to reconciliation for the pain and suffering that they have caused their victims and the family members of their victims. Although Genzo's victims could not be brought back, their families were given some form of closure knowing that the man who committed the cruel acts faced the ultimate justice.

Whether you believe in the death penalty or not, the one thing that Japanese and global society will forever agree on is that Genzo Kurita left behind a dark legacy that will forever continue to shock people to the core.

Appreciation

Thank you to my editor, proofreaders, and cover artist for your support:

Aeternum Designs (book cover); Bettye McKee (editor); Katherine McCarthy, Robyn MacEachern, Linda Howrie, Kathi Garcia, Sandra Miller, Linda Bergeron, Valarie Kiefe, Ron Steed, and Lee Husemann

   ~ RJ

Enjoy this book? You can make a big difference.

Reviews are one of the most powerful tools when it comes to book ranking, exposure and future sales. I have a bunch of loyal readers, and honest reviews of my books help bring them to the attention of other readers.

If you've enjoyed this book, I would be very grateful if you'd take a few minutes to write a brief review on Amazon.

Thank you so much,

RJ

Monthly KINDLE HD FIRE Giveaway

***

Drawing each month on the 30th...

***

Enter to WIN

(No Purchase Necessary)

Click HERE   *http://www.rjparkerpublish-ing.com/Win-a-Kindle.html*

The Staircase

Love. Affection. Romance. Happiness. Care. Kids. Beauty. Trust. Belief -- these are some of the other names when describing the relationship of a husband and wife. Both partners are responsible to make the world beautiful for each other. Whether it's about sharing duties or enjoying the moments, one is incomplete without the other. Or, we can say that the world is nothing if one goes away because there is no one who could take that special person's place.

But what happens when one spouse decides to eliminate the other? What would happen if one decides to live the rest of his/her life with someone else, or alone? That is the time when feelings die and the relationship has no better option but separation. But guess what, if they do have children, *they* would be the real victims since they have to decide with whom they want to live!

This happened with Todd and Clayton Peterson when their parents, Michael and Patricia Peterson, separated. Although they were happy, something went wrong in their relationship, which caused them to go their separate ways. Luckily, Michael found a new partner in Kathleen Atwater, and they were married after dating for some time. Or, unlucky for Kathleen.

Their lives changed when Kathleen Peterson was found dead on the staircase of their Durham mansion. Everything changed. Police claimed that it was a murder and Michael was the prime suspect. (The spouse is usually the number one suspect in any domestic homicide.)

So read this true crime story and get to know about how Michael dealt with the trial, what the evidence was and lacked that found him guilty of murder, and where he is right now. The book is full of interesting plots and twists that actually happened throughout the proceedings.

Background/Personal Life

Michael Peterson is now in his mid-seventies. He lives a quiet life in Durham, North Carolina, and maintains relationships with his two biological children, Clayton and Todd, and their adopted siblings, Margaret and Martha. Most of the rest of his family is estranged.

Michael was born in Nashville, Tennessee, on October 23, 1943, to Eugene (or Eugen) Iver Peterson and Eleanor Peterson nee Bartolino. Michael had one brother, Jack. Eugene was a career military officer, and the family moved frequently. Traveling encouraged Michael to become an avid reader. He hoped to become a celebrated author in the tradition of his favorite author, Ernest Hemingway.

A student of political science at Duke University, Michael was involved in campus activities. He edited the student newspaper, *The Chronicle,* and was president of Sigma Nu Fraternity. He graduated in 1965 and briefly attended law school at the University of North Carolina at Chapel Hill.

In 1965, Michael first got married to Patricia Sue in Durham where she used to teach at an elementary school of the Rhein-Main Air Base near Frankfurt, West Germany. They were blessed with two sons, Clayton and Todd. While living in Germany, the Petersons became close friends with Elizabeth and George Ratliff and their two children, Margaret and Martha. After George died, Elizabeth relied on the Petersons for emotional support. Then, in 1985, Elizabeth died after falling down the stairs in her home in Grafenhausen, and Michael became guardian of the two girls.

Patricia and Michael divorced in 1987. The reasons were unknown, and the couple maintained a congenial relationship after their divorce. Martha and Margaret continued to live with Michael. Clayton and Todd stayed with their mother at first, then moved in with Michael and the girls who had moved to Durham, North Carolina.

Kathleen Hunt Atwater was a neighbor of the Petersons in Durham. Ten years his junior, Kathleen was a leader and prominent citizen in Durham. A divorced mother of one daughter, Caitlin, Kathleen was an executive at Nortel Networks where she received awards for leadership. She traveled for her work to Russia, Ukraine, Vietnam, Malaysia, Europe, Hong Kong, and Canada.

Michael met Kathleen through their children. Caitlin was friends with Martha and Margaret and was thrilled when in 1989, Michael and the children moved in with Kathleen and Caitlin. They were married in 1997. At that time, they lived in a home on Bull City Rising described as being over 9,000 square feet and sitting on 3.5 acres of land. The home had five bedrooms and six bathrooms, plenty of room for the family. Later on, they moved to a Durham mansion of 11,000 square feet with their five children. The family tree of Michael was a bit complicated since it comprises of a lot of people who were not related to him directly.

Caitlin Atwater: Michael's stepdaughter, who was worried about her mother getting married with someone she already knew. She was a friend of Martha and Margaret and, therefore, was feeling a bit confused about her relationship after Michael and Kathleen married. She was very happy when Michael and Kathleen got married since she found nothing but love and affection in their relationship.

Clayton Peterson: Elder son of Patricia and Michael who used to live with Michael after his parents got divorced. He believed that his father was innocent of Kathleen's murder.

Todd Peterson: Second son from Michael's first wife who was always there for Michael's support.

Margaret Ratliff: One of the adopted daughters of George and Elizabeth Ratliff. She also believed that her new father didn't do anything.

Martha Ratliff: Sister of Margaret and a supporter of Michael.

Although Michael was an admitted

bisexual who reportedly had repeated sexual encounters with men throughout their marriage, the children said the marriage was a happy one and the Petersons were excellent parents. After Kathleen's death, Michael was reported as saying, *"Kathleen was my life, I whispered her name in my heart a thousand times, she is there but I can't stop crying."*

The Petersons did have family issues. Clayton Peterson had turbulent teenage years in Germany. He moved to Durham to be with his father, planning to attend Duke University. At the age of 19, however, he was arrested and subsequently convicted of planting a pipe bomb submerged in gasoline in a Duke University administrative office. He admitted to the crime and said he had done it to divert attention from his simultaneous theft of photo identification equipment to make a fake ID. After serving time in prison, Clayton enrolled in North Carolina State University where he became class valedictorian.

Todd Clayton also graduated from NCSU and worked briefly at Nortel Networks, his stepmother's employer. He left, however, to start a website called Futazi.com. The site was a message board for teenagers and offered advice on dating, kissing, sexuality, and friendship. It also had photos of scantily clad high school girls. Todd had an alter ego on this site named "Roman Croft". Croft was a bodybuilder, and the site showed "before" and "after" photos of him in boxer shorts.

The Petersons were active members of the Durham community and, in 1999, Michael ran for Mayor of Durham. He was soundly defeated after questions arose about his credibility. Peterson had served in Vietnam. He claimed several awards including the Bronze Star with Valor and two Purple Hearts. He had no paperwork to back up his medals and later admitted he had received a Purple Heart and Honorable Discharge after a car accident in Japan.

There are signs that the apparently happy Peterson marriage may have been strained. Despite a supposed net worth of over $2 million, they had over $140,000 in credit card debt in 2001. When Martha Ratliff was slated to attend the University of San Francisco, a private college costing $33,000 per year, Michael contacted Martha's paternal uncle to assist with $5,000 each semester. The uncle agreed.

In November 2001, Michael contacted his ex-wife, Patricia, requesting she take out a loan for $30,000 to pay off credit card debt incurred by their sons, Clayton and Todd. Reportedly, he told Patricia that he couldn't discuss the issue with Kathleen.

As to Michael Peterson's bisexuality, it is unclear whether Kathleen knew about his relationships and agreed to them. Michael had at least one confirmed email relationship with a male escort. They had plans to meet in person, but the escort stood him up.

Peterson had served in Vietnam and later wrote several books inspired by his military career and his career in government service. He also worked as a newspaper columnist and became known for his strong political views and his criticism of Durham police and County District Attorney James Hardin Jr. Hardin was to play a much larger role in Peterson's future.

Michael Peterson's future is what this book is about. There are those who would say that Peterson is an intelligent, patriotic, and loving man. Others would say he is a self-involved narcissist with a grandiose sense of self-importance. Perhaps he is both, perhaps neither.

As a Novelist

As an alumnus of Duke University, a veteran of the Vietnamese Marine Corps and, most importantly, a renowned novelist, Michael Peterson was among those people who always remained in the highlights. Before starting to write novels, he was an active and major contributor in the Marine Corps and served with his best for a significant time period. He fought many wars and battles against the enemies and learned a lot about the conflicts between the parties.

Michael, the son of Eugen, received his Bachelor degree in political science from Duke University but, his thirst for education and dedication to learn about law, took him to Chapel Hill, North Carolina's Law School. After completing his education, in 1968, Michael took on his responsibilities in the US Marines Corps. Truth be told, his career life had been full of controversies. He was particularly known for serving during the Vietnam War because he was a person who got permanently disabled due to a car accident in Japan. He fought from that level and regained his confidence to restart his life. With incredible services and efforts, he was honorably given the rank of a Captain, he also claimed a Bronze Star, Silver Star and two purple hearts. But, there was no documentation of his claims.

After he left the Marine Corps, Michael

found his interest in book writing and decided to share his experience in Vietnam. Michael started to list down points and ultimately wrote three books in which he discussed different wars and events he came across throughout his service. He became famous as a novelist due to three novels, namely A Time of War, The Enemy, and The Immortal Dragon, because they were the perfect representation of what he had gone through. These novels discussed everything about the Vietnamese conflict. All three novels were in handwritten form, which were later printed and published officially.

His experience as an Editor of The Duke Chronicle, the student newspaper at Duke University, also helped a lot to make everything work just the right way. Michael was also the co-writer of the Marines of Love Company and the Biographical Charlie Two Shoes with David Perlmutt, the journalist. He also worked for the Durham Herald-Sun as a newspaper columnist. He used to highlight and criticize the Durham police for their inabilities, due to which his columns captured most of the attention and he become popular over time.

After combining the impact, outcomes and experiences of his past life, Michael started a new chapter of his life and began to deliver his thoughts to others. Instead of returning home from the Vietnam War and trying to forget everything, he brought everything on the papers and wrote these detailed, interesting and inspiring novels.

1. *Immortal Dragon*

Finalized and published in 1983, Immortal Dragon is the beginning of Michael's services in the Marine Corps during the Vietnam War. The novel is the perfect representation of what had actually happened during the war. It focuses on the 19th century events when Andre Lafabre came from France to Vietnam in disguise and was caught up in deadly intrigues. He struggled for power and made all efforts to regain his status.

2. *A Time of War*

Published in 1990, this novel is the continuation to his experience in Vietnam. The novelist captures the essence of time. Michael Peterson has written this astounding and richly-textured novel with incredible creativity and knowledge. He discusses the classical story of Vietnam that is blood-chilling, brilliant, compelling and sweeping.

3. *A Bitter Peace*

This sequel of Michael Peterson's war classic about Vietnam revolves around the Presidential thoughts over Bradley Marshall's mission for regaining peace with honor in the country. But unluckily, things did not turn out in the way they are expected, and his efforts turned into failure that would haunt him for years. This novel is full of unremitting suspense and wrenching insight over how a man seeks to achieve his goals and deals with personal redemption.

4. _Charlie Two Shoes and the Marines of Love Company_

Michael co-worked on this novel with David Perlmutt and brought this masterpiece to limelight in 1998. This novel is about an 11-year old Chinese boy, named Tsui Chi-Hsii, who is famous as Charlie Tsuii, his American name. He was approached by a company of US Marines which was transferred to China in 1945 right after World War II ends. He was intended to protect the men of Love Company, from 1st Division, in return for clothing and food. The Marine Division also took the responsibility of his education, but as the communists took charge of China in 1949, Charlie was left alone as the Love Company had to leave the country. Charlie had to suffer and struggle to make both ends meet in China.

While looking at the facts, it's quite evident to say that Michael's popularity as a novelist is still unclear due to his conviction in 2001 for the murder of his second wife, Kathleen Peterson. However, his efforts for Charlie Two Shoes explain the extent of his skills on their own. The way he converted this real-life story into a thrilling and exciting masterpiece is quite remarkable. Even the collection of three books on the Vietnam War is something that readers could not forget and would love to read again and again.

Relationship with Patricia

The relationship of a husband with his wife is one of the most beautiful and trusted realities; that no one could deny. Being a supporting wife of a hard-working husband is what makes the bonding of Michael Peterson and Patricia Sue Peterson stronger. As the famous quote says: *"A man's success is measured by what his wife and children say about him. Money and accomplishments mean nothing if you let your home fail."*

The same goes for Michael Peterson and his family where his first wife used to support him at every stage of life. Even his children had been quite supportive and cooperative. Patricia Peterson was among those women who were always present with their husband.

Whether it was about helping him to write novels or increasing morale to fight against life problems, Patricia had been of great support to Michael Peterson. After their marriage in 1965, the couple was living a beautiful life and received the world's greatest blessings in the form of Todd and Clayton. The family was having a great time together until 1987 when the couple divorced.

After their separation, Michael was performing his responsibilities as the guardian of Martha and Margaret (daughters of his neighbors in Germany, George and Elizabeth

Ratliff) while Todd and Clayton were living with Patricia.

After almost ten years, in 1997, Michael Peterson married Kathleen and began living in Cedar Street Home in Norwalk, California USA. Kathleen also had a daughter named Caitlin. After some time, there were joined by Todd and Clayton, and the extended family started with new aspirations and intentions to live their lives.

Yet, Patricia had a soft spot for Michael due to which she and her sons had been a huge support for Michael when he was convicted of murdering his second wife, Kathleen. She even took part in the hearing and had a clear stance that Michael couldn't do anything like that. After living so many years with him, she was quite certain he was innocent and would say that she had believed in him and would until her last breath.

Patricia was even certain about Michael and Kathleen's relationship as husband and wife. At one occasion, she said that she knew everything about their married life and was quite happy to see them together. Although they hardly talked with each other, their bond with the children was as strong and trustworthy as it should be.

Kathleen Peterson

After being separated from Patricia in 1987, Michael began to live alone and had focused on his career more than before. He became quite serious about what he was doing. He dedicated many years to himself and tried to explore new opportunities in order to pursue his career accordingly. After living alone for a few years, he met Kathleen Hunt Atwater who was a widow and mother of a girl named Caitlin Atwater. They became really good friends and showed complete interest in each other.

Kathleen was born on February 21, 1953, in Greensboro, North Carolina. Kathleen was quite a dedicated and enthusiastic individual about her dreams and initially decided to complete her studies in engineering while she also showed incredible leadership qualities. Since Michael was, himself, a successful and career-oriented person, he was inspired by Kathleen's professional journey from her school to college. He used to appreciate her for being an active contributor at school, where she performed her responsibilities as the President of the Debating Club along with fulfilling her duties as an Editor for the 'Generation' school magazine.

Kathleen received her BS degree in civil engineering and pursued her Master's in mechanical engineering from Duke University.

Michael and Kathleen were quite

identical with respect to their dedication towards making their careers successful and brighter. Kathleen received many leadership awards while Michael was a renowned fiction novelist.

They were married in 1997 and moved in at 1810 Cedar Street, a suburb of Durham in North Carolina. The 48-year-old woman was living her life to the fullest and was working a perfect job at Nortel as a Business Executive, while her personal life was also doing great. However, for her, the real accomplishment was her family, which she created and raised with a lot of love and affection. Kathleen always had complete support from her love and best friend Michael, along with their children, Caitlin, Todd, Clayton, Margaret and Martha. Even Kathleen's mother in Florida (Veronica Hunt), sisters living in Virginia (Lori Campbell and Candace Zamperini) and brother in Tennessee (Steven Hunt) were also there to help and support her.

*****

The Petersons were living an above-average life. Their 11,000-square-foot mansion is the masterpiece of Chinese trinkets and artwork, particularly their huge living room that shows off their style sense and knowledge about how to incorporate antique items into their home.

Bright sunlight streams into the rooms from amazingly installed bay windows that is reflected by glass-covered photographs of Kathleen and Michael's wedding. Everything in their three-story mansion seems to be in complete harmony with the surroundings.

Their life was going so simple and enjoyable with their five children that they never thought of becoming the subject of one of the most mysterious and baffling true crime stories, featured as '*The Staircase Murders*.'

*****

During the early hours of December 9, 2001, Kathleen Peterson was found dead on the blood-stained staircase of their mansion. The evidence on the hardwood floor boards and salmon-colored walls explained the entire story of how badly she had fallen. The amount of blood on the staircase seemed to be quite inconsistent, which was giving a different impression from what had been told to the police initially. Even the actual and confirmed time of death was different from what Michael told the 911 operator. The investigators also uncovered extramarital dalliances and referred to the similarities between Kathleen's death and another stairway fall of their close friend's wife. These initial discoveries were pointing to Michael as the major suspect since there was so much deviation between his statements and the actual findings.

Aphrodite Jones wrote a book on Michael's role as the husband, titled '*A Perfect Husband*,' in which Michael talked about a case that was similar to what happened to Kathleen that night. In that case, the battle led to some legal allegations that turned out to be one of the longest proceedings in Tennessee history. The same excerpts were found in the Kathleen Peterson death case when some strong evidences pointed to Michael for manipulating information. His call to 911 was suspicious as if he was trying to cover his role in her death. However, there was another perception that he was shocked and scared after seeing his wife that way and, therefore, he said whatever came in his mind first.

*****

It was 2:40 AM on December 9, 2001, when a frantic and shocked man dialed 911 to ask for help in an emergency. He was breathing heavily while reporting the incident to Durham police in North Carolina that his wife fell down the stairs at their Cedar Street home. The caller reported that she had an accident and was still breathing. Their conversation after reporting the crime is as follows:

9-1-1 Operator: Okay, how many stairs did she fall down?

Caller: What? Huh?

9-1-1 Operator: How many stairs?

Caller: Stairs?

9-1-1 Operator: How many stairs?

Caller: Ah . . . Oh . . .

9-1-1 Operator: Calm down, sir. Calm down.

According to the operator, the caller was really confused and kept saying that his wife was unconscious. He was asking for the emergency crew to arrive with help immediately. He provided the address, but the operator was a bit unsure about how to calm him down. She was having difficulty in understanding what he was saying. He was breathing hard while his voice was so shrill that it was hard to understand a single word. She assured him that help would be there within a few minutes. He just had to calm down and answer some important questions:

9-1-1 Operator: Calm down, sir. Calm down. How many stairs did she fall down?

Caller: Oh, fifteen, twenty. I don't know. Please get somebody here right away. Please!

9-1-1 Operator: Sir, somebody else is dispatching the ambulance.

Caller: It's in Forest Hills, okay? Please! Please!

9-1-1- Operator: Okay. Is she awake now? Hello? Hello?

There was no reply from the caller, but she could hear him yelling '*Oh God!*' in the background, and then, no connection! The operator immediately dialed Engine 5, Medic 5 to alert the emergency crew. She directly transferred information to the rescue team and sent them to the Cedar Street home address. As soon as she completed her radio call with the team, there was another emergency call ringing on 911.

9-1-1 Operator: Durham 911, what is your emergency?

Caller: Where are they? Why is she not breathing? Please! Please, would you hurry up!

The caller was able to hear a static voice from the background as if someone was talking with the radio operators and yelling Code 5. The caller was getting frantic with every passing second, but there was no reply to the operator's words:

9-1-1 Operator: Sir? Hello? Hello?

Eight minutes later, the rescue team was able to find the place on Cedar Street because they took a wrong turn in the wooded neighborhood. All the lights in the house were on that time, and the paramedics immediately rushed into the home and found the victim on the stairs. She had no pulse.

Officers Figueroa and McDowell from Durham Police Department soon arrived at the scene and began their investigation. Police then went ahead and attempted to identify the caller, but he was so shocked and hysterical that he wasn't able to control himself from crying.

What Officers Said About the Scene

According to Officer Figueroa, as he arrived at the Cedar Street Home, it was 2:50 A.M. and everything seemed to be quite mysterious and troublesome. The victim, Kathleen Atwater Peterson, was lying at the bottom of the stairs in a pool of blood with her head against the stairwell. There were also male athletic shoes beside her with a pair of flip-flop sandals and white socks. What caught the officer's attention was the roll of paper towels soaked in blood.

At 3:07 A.M., Figueroa was joined by Dan George, Durham Investigator, along with other patrol cars and fire trucks which were sent to inspect the back entryway to the residence. George intentionally walked through the scene and instructed Figueroa to secure the residence before moving on with his investigation. Since the mansion was quite huge, they asked for more backup in order to cover the entire space within a short time period. On his initial analysis, he reported that there was blood everywhere, especially on the walls and several steps leading to the stairway. Both officers waited until the Crime Investigation Department (CID) reached the place.

As soon as he met the investigation team, George mentioned that there was something wrong with the scene. Following his lead, the investigation team began following the evidence and headed to the kitchen door where Michael Peterson was standing, dressed in a T-shirt and shorts. He was also covered in blood. His son Todd was also present behind him as he was trying to console Michael. He was constantly mentioning to check Kathleen's body. Just a few minutes later, Michael rushed towards his wife, bent down, cried and caressed her. His actions were so immediate that no officer had a chance to prevent him from touching her body and probably further contaminating the questionable crime scene.

After trying on their own with no results, they asked Todd to help his father move away from her body. But, unfortunately, the damage was already done and the evidence was not there in the actual form. Michael managed to transfer bloodstains on his body as well, thus making it more difficult for forensics.

Not only such actions made him suspicious, but Dan George also noticed a civilian, a young lady named Christina Tomasetti, the daughter of Michael's best friend. George questioned her presence in the kitchen. Christina stated that she was with Todd at a party and had just arrived when the fire trucks reached the crime scene.

As soon as the officers followed the instructions to seal the scene, two more people, Ben Maynard and Heather Whitson, approached from out of nowhere. They had been called by Todd for help because they were in the neighborhood. Todd specifically told Ben to bring Heather because she was a medical student at Duke University and knew how to help his father to come out of shock.

As they arrived at the scene, Durham Police were not likely to let them enter the home but, upon Todd's request, they eventually allowed them to enter. Todd took them around the staircase and entered into the kitchen through the fine dining room. All of them consoled Mr. Peterson and made all efforts to take him out of the trauma. But nothing was working as he couldn't bear the pain of such a big loss, his wife. He refused to accept any medical care and wanted to be left alone.

Michael kept mumbling that he couldn't

live without his beloved wife! He recapped the entire day of December 9, 2001:

Michael and Kathleen were enjoying a few drinks as part of their celebration.

They were having a great time together.

Michael, then, went towards the pool area and took the dogs to spend some time with them as well.

He thought that Kathleen was upstairs going to bed, but never thought of seeing something like that.

Considering his father's grief and sadness, Todd asked the uniformed officers if he could take a look at his stepmom's body a bit closer. They granted him permission to do so, and as he knelt down, he touched her legs and found no signs of life. Then, with the help of a flashlight, everyone paid attention to Kathleen's injured head and found something wrong at the blood around her body and clothes. As well, there were bruises and a strange pained look on her face.

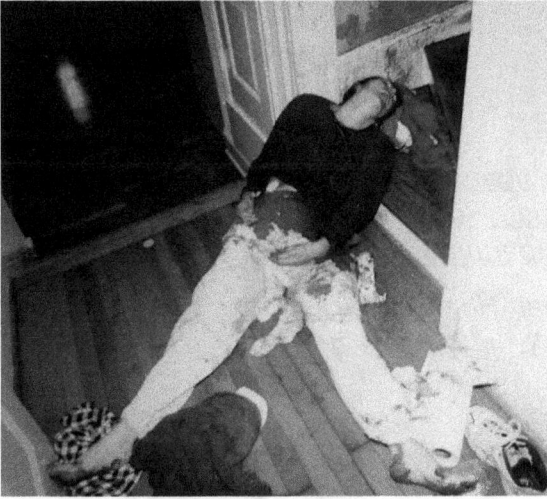

According to the Witness, Fran Borden:

As soon as he arrived at the 1810 Cedar Street home on December 9, 2001, Sergeant Borden was instructed to investigate a woman's death who was reported to have fallen down the staircase. Upon his arrival, his attention was caught by the blood stains on a kitchen cabinet and a drawer handle. As per his later statement to the jurors, that was the *first of the three red flags'.*

Read for FREE using your Kindle Unlimited or BUY NOW

Amazon US

Amazon UK

Amazon Canada

Books by RJ Parker

Women Who Kill

Beyond Stick and Stones

Cold Blooded Killers

Case Closed: Serial Killers Captured

Radical Islamic Terrorism in America Today

Hell's Angels Biker War

Serial Killer Groupies

Serial Killer Case Files

Blood Money: The Method and Madness of Assassins: Stories of Real Contract Killers

Serial Killers True Crime Anthologies: Volumes 1 – 4

About the Author

RJ Parker, Ph.D., is an award-winning and bestselling true crime author and owner of RJ Parker Publishing, Inc. He has written over 30 true crime books which are available in eBook, paperback and audiobook editions and have sold in over 100 countries. He holds certifications in Serial Crime, Criminal Profiling and a Ph.D. in Criminology.

To date, RJ has donated over 3,000 autographed books to allied troops serving overseas and to our wounded warriors recovering in Naval and Army hospitals all over the world. He also donates to Victims of Violent Crimes Canada.

Contact Information

Author's Email:

AuthorRJParker@gmail.com

Publisher's Email:

Agent@RJParkerPublishing.com

Website:

http://RJPARKERPUBLISHING.com/

Twitter:

http://www.Twitter.com/realRJParker

Facebook:

https://www.Facebook.com/AuthorRJParker

Instagram:

https://Instagram.com/RJParkerPub

Bookbub:

https://www.bookbub.com/authors/rj-parker

Amazon Author's Page:

rjpp.ca/RJ-PARKER-BOOKS

References: Introduction and Stats

1. Aggrawal p.4
2. Herodotus (c. 440 BC). The Histories (Book 2
3. American Psychiatric Association, ed. (2013). "Other Specified Paraphilic Disorder, 302.89 (F65.89)". Diagnostic and Statistical Manual of Mental Disorders, Fifth Edition. American Psychiatric Publishing. p. 705.
4. Rosman, J. P.; Resnick, P. J. (1 June 1989). "Sexual attraction to corpses: A psychiatric review of necrophilia"

The Hong Kong Butcher

1. Li, Jessica (August 13, 2017). "From our archives: the capture of Hong Kong's Jars Killer". South China Morning Post.
2. The Rainy Night killer: Lam Kor-Wan (in Cantonese language)

The Green River Killer

1. Bell, Rachel. "Green River Killer: River of Death". Crime Library.
2. McCarthy, Terry; Thornburgh, Nathan (June 3, 2002). "River Of Death". Time. Retrieved July 20, 2012.
3. Montaldo, Charles (February 14, 2011). "Gary Ridgway: The Green River Killer"
4. Ridgway Reveals Gruesome Details In Chilling Confession". KIRO 7 Eyewitness News
5. "Find An Offender - Ridgway, Gary L". Washington State Department of Corrections.
6. Maleng, Norm (November 5, 2003). "Statement of Norm Maleng on Ridgway Plea
7. "Gary Ridgway, Green River Killer, Charged With Murder #49, but Still Won't Face

Execution"
8. Green, Sarah Jean (23 November 2005). "Remains of a Green River killer victim found near Issaquah
9. "Anitra Mulwee". karisable.com
10. Prothero, M.; Smith, C. (2006). Defending Gary: Unraveling the Mind of the Green River Killer

Edmund Kemper
1. Ressler 1993
2. Seager, Stephen (2014). Behind the Gates of Gomorrah: A Year with the Criminally Insane
3. Brottman, Mikita (2002). Car Crash Culture. pp. 106–107
4. Pitt, Ingrid (2003). Murder, Torture & Depravity
5. Cheney, Margaret (1976), The Co-ed Killer
6. Martingale, Moira (1995), Cannibal Killers: The History of Impossible Murderers
7. Vronsky, Peter (2004), Serial Killers: The Method and Madness of Monsters
8. Lawson 2002
9. Ascoine, Frank; Lockwood, Randall (1998)
10. Cheney 1976
11. Clarke, Phil. Extreme Evil: Taking Crime to the Next Level.
12. Gerritsen, Tess. The Surgeon
13. Scott, Gini Graham (1 January 2007)
14. Ramsland, Katherine. "More Victims" Crime Library. Archived from the original on February 10, 2015.
15. Douglas & Olshaker 1995, p. 153
16. "Murder: No Apparent Motive". IMDb.
17. "The State". June 4, 1985. Retrieved October 21, 2017 – via LA Times
18. Gillespie, Nick; Snell, Lisa (November 1996)
19. Foy, Scott (7 September 2008).

Anthony Merino

1.   Anthony Merino-Necrophilia Case-Available at: https://inmundosednondemundo.wordpress.com/2015/11/28/anthony-merino-necrophilia-case/
2.   Ranker-"14 Facts about necrophilia that (weirdly) might change your mind about it by Jacob Shelton- Available at: https://www.ranker.com/list/crazy-necrophilia-facts/jacob-shelton/page 2
3.   Digital Journal-"Sex with corpse earns Lab Technician prison time" by Debra Myers- Available at: http://www.digitaljournal.com/article/259708
4.   ABC News- "Cops: Man caught in hospital necrophilia act" by David Schoetz- Available at: http://abcnews.go.com/US/story/id=3794389

Genzo Kurita

Listverse-"Disturbing cases of necrophilia"-Available at: https://listverse.com/2016/07/19/10-disturbing-cases-of-necrophilia/

1-   Wikipedia-"Capital punishment in Japan"-Available at: https://en.wikipedia.org/wiki/Capital_punishment_in_Japan

2-   Google books -" Murder Under the Rising Sun: 15 Japanese Serial Killers that Terrified a Nation" by William Webb-Available at: https://books.google.co.zw/books/id=PY1JAQAAQBAJ&pg=PT22&lpg=PT22&dq=genzo+kurita+murders&source=bl&ots=DhGw3L6nJE&sig=-OU0lKJlFMK8jer7z9YMhjGS0mY&hl=en&sa=X&ved=0ahUKEwiP7-Hgo5HZAhVNa1AKHdy0D4UQ6AEIVDAK#v=onepage&q=genzo%20kurita%20murders&f=false